D.I.Y. MAKE IT HAPPEN

NEIGHBORHOOD CLEANUP

VIRGINIA LOH-HAGAN

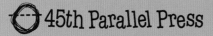
45th Parallel Press

Published in the United States of America by Cherry Lake Publishing
Ann Arbor, Michigan
www.cherrylakepublishing.com

Reading Adviser: Marla Conn MS, Ed., Literacy specialist, Read-Ability, Inc.
Book Designer: Felicia Macheske

Photo Credits: © oumjeab/Shutterstock.com, cover, 1; © Mike Truchon/Shutterstock.com, cover, 1; © rangizzz/Shutterstock.com, cover, 1; © bnamfa/Shutterstock.com, 3; © mangostock/Shutterstock.com, 5; © Beth Van Trees/Shutterstock.com, 7; © Lev Kropotov/Shutterstock.com, 7; © Byron W.Moore/Shutterstock.com, 9; © photka/Shutterstock.com, 10; © Dmitry Kalinovsky/Shutterstock.com, 11; © Pavel Kubarkov/Shutterstock.com, 12; © MAHATHIR MOHD YASIN/Shutterstock.com, 14, 31; © Lisa F. Young/Shutterstock.com, 15; © wavebreakmedia/Shutterstock.com, 17, back cover; © Blaj Gabriel/Shutterstock.com, 18; © Meister Photos/Shutterstock.com, 20; © Jake Rennaker/Shutterstock.com, 21, 31; © Dragon Images/Shutterstock.com, 22; © COLOA Studio/Shutterstock.com, 23; © monticello/Shutterstock.com, 25; © Rawpixel.com/Shutterstock.com, 28; © michaeljung/Shutterstock.com, 29

Graphic Elements Throughout: © pashabo/Shutterstock.com; © axako/Shutterstock.com; © IreneArt/Shutterstock.com; © Katya Bogina/Shutterstock.com; © Belausava Volha/Shutterstock.com; © Nik Merkulov/Shutterstock.com; © Ya Tshey/Shutterstock.com; © kubais/Shutterstock.com; © Sasha Nazim/Shutterstock.com; © Infomages/Shutterstock.com; © Ursa Major/Shutterstock.com; © topform/Shutterstock.com; © Art'nLera/Shutterstock.com; © tanvetka/Shutterstock.com; © Natasha Pankina/Shutterstock.com; © Fandorina Liza/Shutterstock.com

45th Parallel Press is an imprint of Cherry Lake Publishing.

Library of Congress Cataloging-in-Publication Data has been filed and is available at catalog.loc.gov

Cherry Lake Publishing would like to acknowledge the work of The Partnership for 21st Century Skills.
Please visit *www.p21.org* for more information.

Printed in the United States of America
Corporate Graphics

ABOUT THE AUTHOR

Dr. Virginia Loh-Hagan is an author, university professor, former classroom teacher, and curriculum designer. She doesn't like cleaning her house. But she loves doing community service. She lives in San Diego with her very tall husband and very naughty dogs. To learn more about her, visit www.virginialoh.com.

TABLE OF CONTENTS

CHAPTER ONE

WHAT DOES IT MEAN TO PLAN A NEIGHBORHOOD CLEANUP?

Do you love helping? Do you love cleaning? Do you love your neighborhood? Then, organize a neighborhood cleanup. It's the right project for you!

Neighborhoods are where people live. People want a clean area. But not all areas are clean. Some people litter. Litter means to drop trash on the ground. Some people **tag** walls. Tag means to spray paint. Some people **neglect** their spaces. Neglect means to not take care of. Some neighborhoods need to be cleaned up.

One person can clean up a small area.
But it would be hard to clean a big area.
That's why people organize cleanup events.

Talk to other organizers. Get
their opinions.

KNOW THE LINGO

Conservation: the protection, improvement, and use of natural resources

Greenbelt: an area of natural land around urban areas

Hardscape: man-made features added to a natural landscape, like walkways and walls

Leachate: liquids that come in contact with waste

Open space: a cleared area in or near a city

Ordinances: city laws

Roll-offs: dumpsters on wheels

Rural: farm area

Sanitation: waste disposal services

Softscape: the natural elements of an area, like plants and trees

Suburban: area outside of a city with many homes

Urban: city area with businesses and apartments

Zoning: land areas for specific purposes

Neighborhood cleanups are events. People meet up. They work together. They bring the area back to life. They clean. They wash. They pick up litter. They get rid of trash.

Cleanup events make people feel good. They help people feel pride. People complete a task. They see the results of their work. They see a clean neighborhood. This is good for everyone.

These events build teamwork. They build a sense of community. They bring people together.

You'll plan. You'll make new friends. You'll serve the community. You'll keep communities clean. The best part is you'll have fun!

Introduce yourself to new people.

CHAPTER TWO

WHAT DO YOU NEED TO PLAN A NEIGHBORHOOD CLEANUP?

Choose a place.

➡ Choose an area that needs to be cleaned.

➡ Study trash pickup routes. Routes are paths. Choose an area around these routes. It'll be easier. City trash services can help pick up some trash.

➡ Consider places that many people go. Examples are parks and roads. These places improve neighborhoods.

Choose a time.

➡ **Host during the day. People see better in the day. It's safer during the day.**

➡ **Study weather reports. Choose a nice day. Avoid rain and snow.**

➡ **Consider hosting in spring. This is before grass and weeds grow. Grass and weeds hide trash.**

➡ **Start planning a month before.**

Check to see what other events are on your chosen date.

Talk to city **officials**. Officials are people in charge of things.

➡ **Get permits**. Permits give permission to do something. Cleanup events include large groups of people. These people meet in public places. Some cities require permits to use public places.

➡ **Talk to waste disposal officials**. Waste is trash. Disposal means getting rid of. These people provide trash and recycling services.

➡ **Ask where trash should be dumped. Ask how trash should be dumped.**

➡ **Reserve haulers**. Haulers are **dumpsters** with wheels. Dumpsters are large trash bins. This is where people put trash. The city takes trash away to **landfills**. Landfills are places where trash is buried and covered up.

Follow city rules about waste disposal.

Get supplies. These are things needed for the cleanup. See if you can get items donated. See if you can borrow items.

➡ Get matching T-shirts. Have all **volunteers** wear these shirts. Volunteers are people who give up their time to do good deeds.

➡ Provide trash bags. People collect trash. They place it in bags.

➡ Get dumpsters. Get one for trash. Get one for recycling.

➡ Get gardening tools. Examples are rakes and clippers. Some areas need lawn mowers.

➡ Get trash collectors. These are tools. They pick up trash. They're called pickers.

➡ Get carts with wheels. These can carry heavy things.

➡ Get drinks and snacks. People get hungry. People get thirsty.

Get ties for the bags.

TRY THIS!

Make the cleanup event more exciting. Plan a "Jail and Bail" contest. This will turn the cleanup into a game.

You'll need: community leaders (student council members, teachers, coaches, parents), bags of trash, a jail area

Steps

1 Create a jail. Use a big cardboard box. Or block off an area. Put a "Jail" sign over it.

2 Ask community leaders to participate. Put them in the jail area.

3 Set "bail." For each person, state a number of bags. This is the number of bags needed to get them out of jail.

4 Challenge people to collect trash. Tell them to bring full bags of trash.

5 Let leaders go as soon as the bags are turned in.

Keep everyone safe. Things could happen.

➡ Get **first aid** training. People may fall. They may get hurt. First aid helps with cuts. It helps with scrapes. It works until medical help comes.

➡ Get a first aid kit. It has bandages. It has healing creams. It has cleaners. It has eye-washing water.

➡ Get **emergency** training. An emergency is when something dangerous happens. An example is breaking bones.

➡ Get a medical person. Examples are doctors or nurses. Make sure someone is there.

Get safety vests if working by streets.

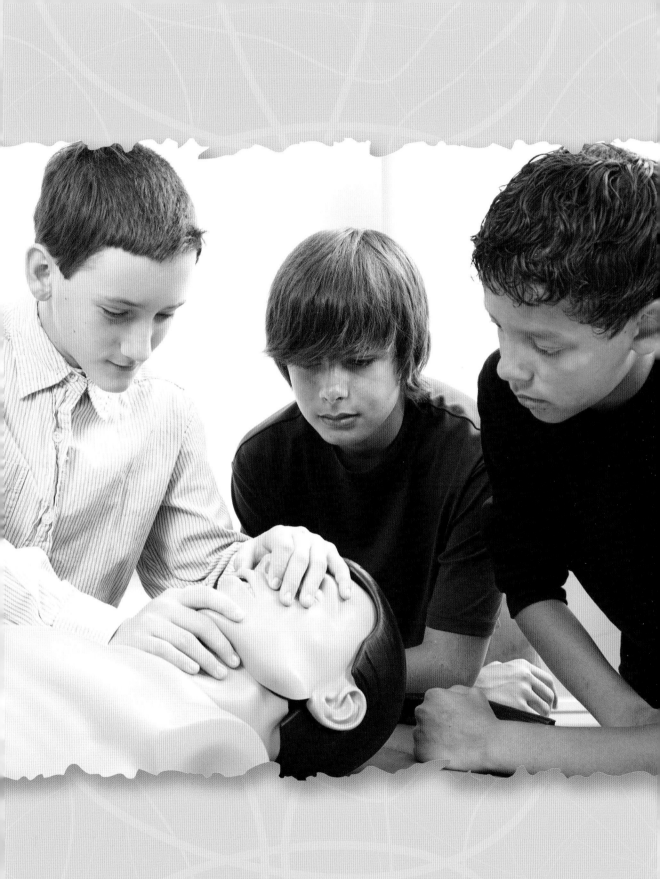

CHAPTER THREE

HOW DO YOU SET UP A NEIGHBORHOOD CLEANUP?

Get volunteers. Promote your event. You need a lot of people. Cleanup events depend on people.

- **Create a Web site. Include information about your event. Include a way for people to sign up.**

- **Use social media. Post about your event. Build interest.**

- **Make a flyer. Flyers are information on paper. Post flyers around town.**

- **Work with community groups. Partner with other people. Join forces. Many people want to help their communities.**

➡ **Ask family and friends. Tell everyone about your event.**

➡ **Talk to business owners. Ask them for donations. Donations are gifts.**

Invite people of all ages.

MIGUEL ANGEL ALDRETE

Miguel Angel Aldrete is from Chula Vista, California. He wants to help the environment. He wants to help the poor. He wants to help his community. He founded Kids 4 Our World. He did this when he was 8 years old. His group now has over 100 "ambassadors." He provides students with community service opportunities. He said, "As we get older, they will go out and influence other people." His group has volunteered many community service hours. Aldrete advises to give back to the community. He said, "You don't have to be an adult or famous to make a difference in the world." His mission is to make a positive impact for future generations.

What other ways can you think of to help make the world a better place?

Prepare volunteers for the cleanup event.

➡ Tell people to wear good shoes. Shoes should cover toes.

➡ Tell people to wear gloves.

➡ Tell people to protect against sun damage. Wear a hat. Wear sunscreen. Wear sunglasses.

➡ Tell people to protect against bugs. Wear a long shirt. Wear long pants. Use bug spray.

Get volunteers to sign **consent** forms. Consent means permission.

➡ Ask for names.

➡ Ask for ages.

➡ Ask for **contact information**. This includes addresses. This includes phone numbers.

➡ Ask for an **emergency contact**. This is a person to call if there's trouble. Be prepared.

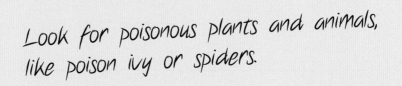

Look for poisonous plants and animals, like poison ivy or spiders.

Know the **risks**. Risks are possible dangers. There are two types.

➡ **General risks** are related to the site. This includes weather. This includes traffic. This includes the area.

➡ **Materials** risks are related to things. This includes trash.

Study the site.

➡ Find the best place for parking. Plan how to control traffic.

➡ Find the best place for collecting trash. Create maps. Mark areas where people can go. Mark areas where they can't go.

➡ Find the best place to sort trash. Plan placements of trash cans. Plan placements of dumpsters.

➡ Plan pickup sites. This is where trash is picked up.

➡ Find the best place for people to meet.

➡ Find the bathrooms.

Keep everyone safe.

➡ **Get a spill kit. This protects against dangerous spills.**

➡ **Bring cat litter. Put it on toxic liquids. Cat litter soaks up the poison.**

➡ **Get safety experts. They handle toxic trash.**

➡ **Tell people not to pick up toxic things. Make a list of toxic items. Give it to all volunteers.**

Wear protective clothing.

There are many examples of toxic trash.

➡ **Paint**

➡ **Cleaning supplies**

➡ **Used batteries**

➡ **Broken glass**

➡ **Needles**

➡ **Knives**

➡ **Electronics**

Have safety experts sort out toxic trash. Don't put it with the regular trash. Don't touch these items.

CHAPTER FOUR

HOW DO YOU RUN A NEIGHBORHOOD CLEANUP?

The big day has come! You've got a date. You've got a site. You've got volunteers!

Use your helpers.

➡ **Put someone in charge of volunteers.**

➡ **Put someone in charge of traffic.**

➡ **Put someone in charge of trash disposal.**

➡ **Put someone in charge of safety.**

Create aid stations. They're special centers.
They provide help.

➡ **Set up tables. Set them up around the cleanup site.**

➡ **Get helpers. Have them work at each station.**

➡ **Provide snacks. Provide drinks.**

➡ **Have first aid kits ready.**

Gather everyone together.

➡ **Get people excited.**

➡ **Organize teams. Assign a team leader.**

➡ **Assign teams to specific areas.**

➡ **Give out supplies.**

Don't do everything yourself.

QUICK TIPS

- Tell people not to trespass. Trespassing is being on someone's property without permission.

- Make a station for people to wash their hands. Provide hand wipes. Provide antibacterial hand gel.

- Beautify your community. Add plants. Build a community garden.

- Look by roadsides. This is where people throw their fast-food trash. This is the most common trash found in cleanup events.

- Tie up loose papers. Papers can fly away.

- Ask an environmental expert to visit your school. Learn more about the harmful impact of litter.

- Make school lunches that don't create trash. Use containers instead of bags. Challenge others to do the same.

- Visit a recycling center. Visit a landfill. See how trash is managed.

Explain the rules.

- Tell people to avoid toxic trash. Tell them to be careful with glass and metal.

- Tell people where the dumpsters are. Make sure they know where to put trash. Make sure they know where to put recycling.

- Tell people not to make more trash.

- Tell people not to work alone. Tell them to be safe.

Participate in the cleanup event.

- Help by cleaning up.

- Be available to help others.

- Be available to solve problems.

End the event.

- Make sure trash is collected.

- Follow up with city officials.

- Clean up after your volunteers.

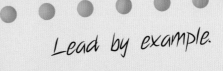

Lead by example.

Thank your volunteers.

➡ **Host a party. This can be a picnic.**

➡ **Write thank-you notes.**

➡ **Invite them to future events.**

Consider making the event more exciting.

➡ **Hide prizes for people to find. Put prizes in plastic eggs. Hide them around the cleanup site. Keep track of the eggs. Make sure you get them all back. Don't make more trash.**

➡ **Give a prize to the person who fills the most trash bags. Think of other ways to win prizes.**

➡ **Give a ticket for every bag. Have people write their names on the ticket. Collect the tickets. Put them in a bag. Pull out names. Give out prizes.**

Think about what worked and what didn't work.

D.I.Y. EXAMPLE!

STEPS	EXAMPLES
Place	Neighborhood school and park
Time	Saturday morning
Recruit volunteers	• Create flyer. Post at school. Post at park. Post at library. • Send flyer. E-mail to friends. E-mail to family. • Ask local radio stations to announce event.
Stations	• Check-In Station: This is where people check in. They get their supplies here. Supplies include a shirt, trash bags, and trash pickers. • Aid Station: This is where people can get first aid. This is where they can get drinks and snacks. • Trash Station: This is where people can dump their trash bags. • Recycling Station: This is where people can dump recycling. • Safety Station: This is where people can report toxic trash. Safety experts will go get the items.

STEPS	EXAMPLES
Challenge	Read the 45th Parallel Press book about scavenger hunts. Create a scavenger hunt. Have volunteers search for items. Give prizes to people who collect all the items. Here are some examples: • Something a kid would throw away • Something an adult would throw away • Something from another country • Something that can be worn
Create schedule of events	• Welcome and introductions • Explanation of event rules and procedures • Cleanup • Awards ceremony • Picnic celebration

GLOSSARY

consent (kuhn-SENT) permission

contact information (KAHN-takt in-fur-MAY-shuhn) personal information including name, address, and phone number

disposal (dis-POH-zuhl) the process of getting rid of something

donations (doh-NAY-shuhnz) gifts

dumpster (DUMP-stur) large trash bin

emergency (ih-MUR-juhn-see) when something dangerous happens

emergency contact (ih-MUR-juhn-see KAHN-takt) the person to call in case of an emergency

first aid (FURST AYD) helping to heal cuts and scrapes before medical help can be provided

flyer (FLYE-ur) information on paper

haulers (HAWL-urz) dumpsters on wheels

landfills (LAND-filz) places where trash is buried and covered up

materials (muh-TEER-ee-uhlz) supplies

neglect (nih-GLEKT) not taking care of something or someone

officials (uh-FISH-uhlz) people in charge of things

permits (PER-mits) licenses giving permission

risks (RISKS) possible dangers

routes (ROOTS) paths

tag (TAG) to spray paint on public property

volunteers (vah-luhn-TEERZ) people who donate their time to help the community

waste (WAYST) trash

INDEX

LEARN MORE

BOOKS

Clinton, Chelsea. *It's Your World: Get Informed, Get Inspired & Get Going!* New York: Philomel Books, 2015.

EarthWorks Group. *The New 50 Simple Things Kids Can Do to Save the Earth.* Kansas City, MO: Andrews McMeel Publishing, 2009.

Jankeliowitch, Anne, and Yann Arthus-Bertrand (photographer). *Kids Who Are Changing the World.* Naperville, IL: Sourcebooks Jabberwocky, 2014.

WEB SITES

Do Something: https://www.dosomething.org

EnviroLink—Earth Day Event Ideas: http://earthday.envirolink.org/guide6.html

WikiHow—How to Organise a Community Clean Up: www.wikihow.com/Organise-a-Community-Clean-Up